Jesus and Me Activity Book

Written by Darlene Hoffa
Illustrated by Kathy Mitter

CPH®
Concordia Publishing House

Copyright © 1996 Concordia Publishing House
3558 S. Jefferson Avenue, St. Louis, MO 63118-3968
Manufactured in the United States of America

3   4   5   6   7   8   9   10   05 04 03 02 01 00 99 98

When Jesus lived on earth, He traveled about sharing the Good News that He is our Savior from sin. While healing, touching, listening, and teaching, Jesus shared His message of God's love. Color the picture. Cut out the picture and circle and glue them to cardboard. Use a paper fastener to attach Jesus to the circle. Make Jesus "walk" and say "God loves you" to your family and friends.

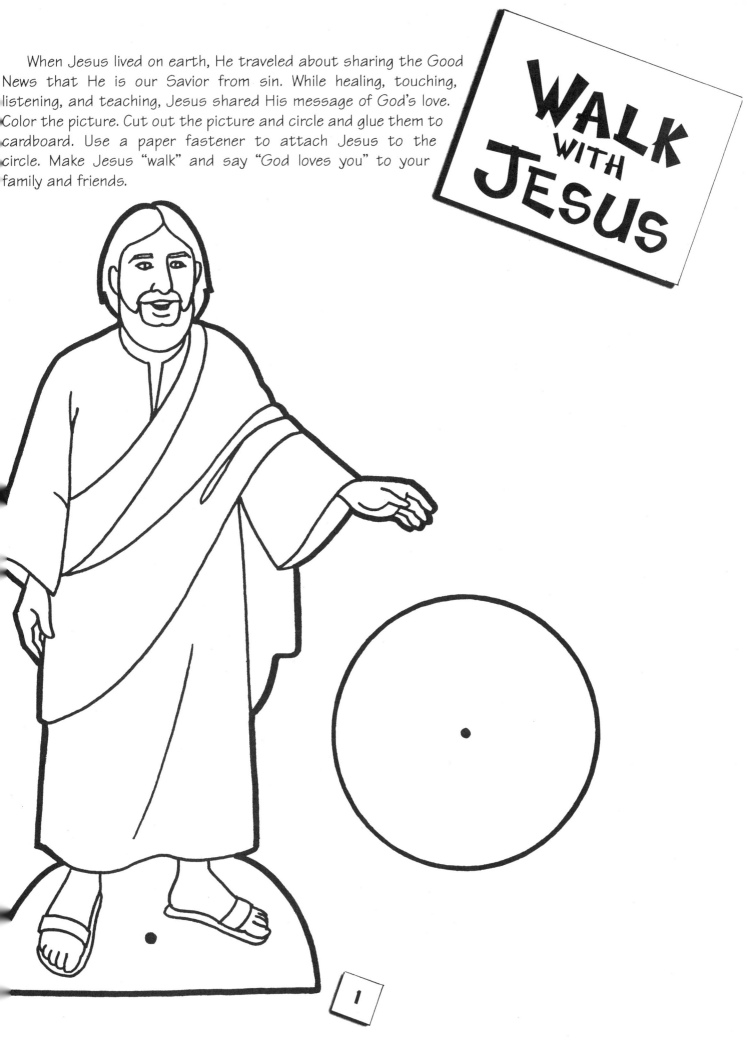

WALK WITH JESUS

1

FOLLOW JESUS' EXAMPLE

Learn what Jesus will help you to do. Use this code to find the secret message. Jesus invites you to live a life filled with love. The activities in this book will show you some fun ways to say "Jesus and I love you" to your family and friends.

A	B	C	D	E	F	G	H	I	J	K	L	M
1	2	3	4	5	6	7	8	9	10	11	12	13

N	O	P	Q	R	S	T	U	V	W	X	Y	Z
26	25	24	23	22	21	20	19	18	17	16	15	14

__ __ __ __   __ __ __ __   __ __ __ __ __
12 25 18 5   5 1 3 8   25 20 8 5 22

__ __ __   __ __ __ __   __ __ __ __ __
1 21 9   8 1 18 5   12 25 18 5 4

__ __ __ .   __ __ __ __   __ __ __ : __ __ __ __
15 25 19   10 25 8 26   A E A B

2

We can read Jesus' words in the Bible. Jesus calls us to Him. He tells us not to be afraid. He promises to always be with us. Use the large heart as a pattern to cut four large hearts from red paper. Cut out the smaller hearts and glue each one to a large heart. Glue or tape the hearts on a piece of ribbon to make a wall decoration.

HEAR JESUS' WORDS

Come to Me.

Do not fear.

Only believe.

You are My friend.

3

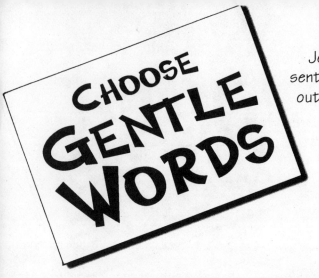

CHOOSE GENTLE WORDS

Jesus will help you use gentle words like He did. Read each sentence. Color the hearts by the words Jesus would say. Cross out the unkind words and change them to kind words.

♡ Let's play.
♡ I like you.
♡ You are dumb.
♡ You can ride first.
♡ Go away.
♡ I feel happy with you.
♡ You can't share my snack.
♡ Let's be friends.
♡ Come back again soon.
♡ You are fun to play with.

When Jesus was a boy, He helped Mary and Joseph. What chores do you think He did? Could He have swept sawdust in Joseph's carpenter shop? Did He help Mary carry water from the well?

You can be a happy helper like Jesus. Draw a line between each job and the way you can help. What would happen if you matched the wrong jobs and washed the cat or raked the dishes? Think of other ways to help at home and at school.

HELP LITTLE CHILDREN

Mothers brought their children to see Jesus. "Shoo! Go away!" Jesus' helpers scolded.

"Let the children come," Jesus said. "Everyone should love and trust God like they do." Then Jesus hugged the little ones and blessed them.

You can show Jesus' love to a little child. Help a little child color these pictures and play the game. Use raisins or cereal circles to mark the path to Grandma's house. Talk about the animals and places you pass along the way.

GRANDMA'S HOUSE

6

One day Jesus talked to a big crowd of people all day long. The people got hungry. The disciples had no food for them. A little boy let Jesus share his lunch. Jesus blessed the boy's lunch. It grew and grew until there was enough to feed everyone and have leftovers too. Jesus helps us share His love by sharing our things with others.

Find these things to share in the letters below.

PAIL SWING   PAINTS SANDWICH

DOG KITTEN BAT BALL BICYCLE

A J H O T Z B P L D
C R I N G E V A M O
K D Q F S S W I N G
W O L B P A X L I T
E A P A I N T S M K
F C X L H D J P S I
V F B L J W Z B A T
K R D A L I B H J T
I N O B I C Y C L E
C J S V M H G J P N

SAY THANK YOU

Jesus healed 10 men who had a sickness called leprosy. Only one man came back to thank Jesus. "Where are the other nine?" Jesus asked.

When we think of all the good gifts Jesus gives to us—especially the gift of His life on the cross for our sins—it is easy to thank Him. He will help us say thank you to our friends and family too.

Make a thank-you card for someone you know. Color the cat and write a thank-you message. Cut out the cat and thank-you message. Fold a piece of construction paper in half. Trace the cat onto the construction paper and cut it out. Glue pieces as shown.

PLACE ON FOLD

Thank You

Thank you for

Love,

_____

CUT OUT AND GLUE INSIDE CARD

Peter wondered how many times he should forgive someone. He asked Jesus if seven times were enough. Jesus said to forgive 77 times! Jesus meant that since He died on the cross to win us forgiveness for all our sins, we should always forgive people when they sin against us.

Follow the directions below to make "I'm sorry" and "I forgive you" puppets. Add hair and eyes made from scraps of construction paper.

①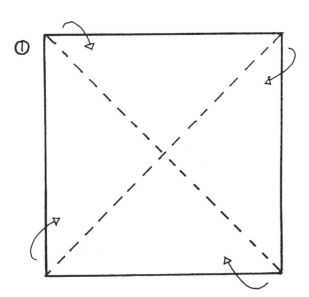

②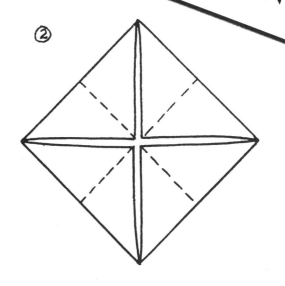

③

Turn over and fold all corners toward the center.

④

Stick thumb and index finger into the created square pockets; press into shape.

⑤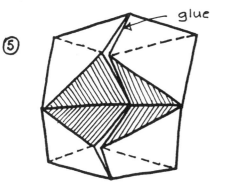

glue

⑥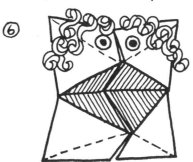

Glue the two sides together.

9

BE A FRIEND

Four men hurried toward a crowded house. Jesus was teaching inside. The men carried their friend on a mat. He could not walk. When the crowd did not budge, the men carried their friend to the roof. They removed some tiles and lowered their friend to Jesus. Jesus forgave the sick man's sins and made him well.

Connect the dots to finish the picture. Think of ways you can be a friend to someone with a disability.

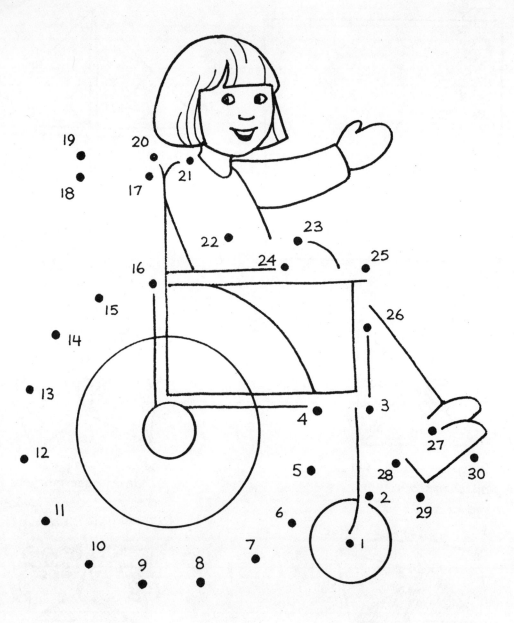

Jesus and His disciples watched as people dropped their money into the offering boxes. Some rich people put in large gifts. Then a poor woman put in two tiny coins. Jesus said that woman gave more than the rich people. She gave all she had, trusting God to care for her.

God gives you so much, and He will help you give Him gifts cheerfully. He will make your small gifts do big things. Write your name and date on the gift. Glue a penny on the star. Draw bright circles around the penny to show God using your gift to do big things. Cut out the pattern and trace it on gift wrap. Fold up the flaps so your gift is inside the gift wrap. Fasten with a sticker or self-adhesive bow.

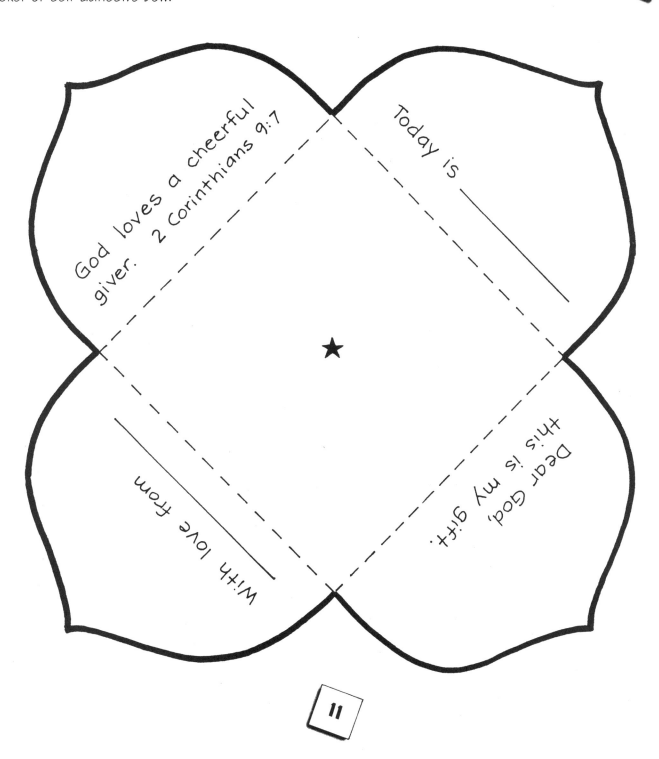

BE A CHEERFUL GIVER

God loves a cheerful giver. 2 Corinthians 9:7

Today is _____

With love from _____

Dear God, this is my gift.

11

LEARN NAMES

Nobody liked Zacchaeus. He made money by cheating people. He climbed high up in a tree to see Jesus pass by. Jesus called, "Zacchaeus, hurry down! I'm coming to your house today."

Jesus knew Zacchaeus' name! Jesus knows your name too. God called you to be His child when you were baptized. Learn the names of new children at your school and church. Say them in a friendly way.

Write your name on the name tag. Then color the children's tags the correct colors.

Hello. My name is

_____

Ryan		Kyle		Lisa		Katy
Katy		Molly		Chris		Molly
Kyle		David		Nicole		Kyle
Lisa		Ryan		Katy		Chris
Molly		Chris		David		Kyle
Chris		Kyle		Ryan		David
Ryan		Katy		Chris		Molly

Color: Chris: red   Lisa: blue
        Molly: yellow   Kyle: brown
        David: green   Katy: orange
        Ryan: purple   Nicole: pink

Jesus told a story about a man who was beaten up by robbers and left on the road. Two church leaders hurried by and did not help the man. A man from Samaria stopped and helped the man and took him to a place to rest. Jesus asks us to be good neighbors to those who need our help.

You can show people God's love by being kind and respectful. Trace the cover pattern on bright construction paper and cut out the window. Cut out the circle with polite words. Use a paper fastener to attach the cover to the circle. Talk about times when you can use these polite words.

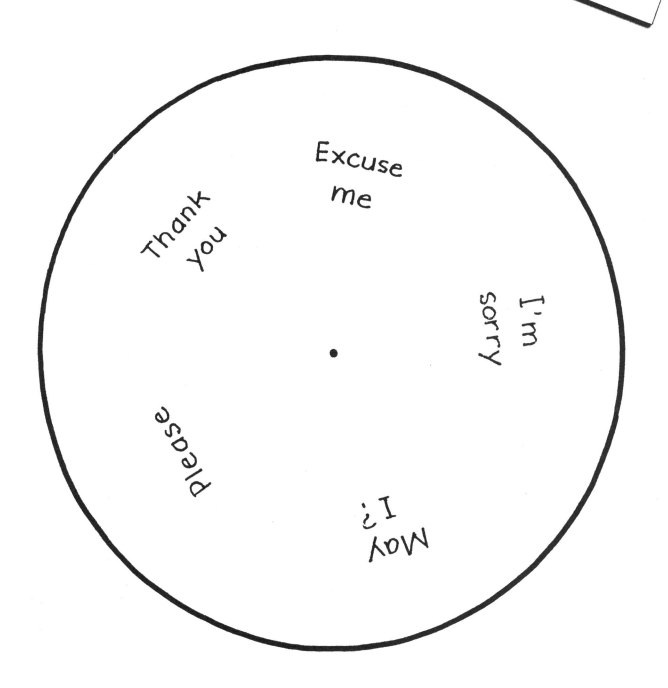

SHOW RESPECT

Excuse me

Thank you

I'm sorry

Please

May I?

cut out

14

Jesus taught His disciples to pray. He taught them to spread the Good News that He would die to pay the price for our sins. He even helped them to fish, and then to catch people for God's kingdom!

Can you teach someone a new skill? Help someone make this secret message spinner. Color the circles. Cut them out and glue them on light cardboard. Glue the two circles together. Punch a hole in each side. Pull a rubber band through each hole and secure it in place. Put your fingers through the rubber bands. Use your fingers and thumbs to wind the circle around and around. Release to see the message "I LOVE YOU" appear as the circle spins. While you work, tell your friend about God's love.

BE A GOOD LISTENER

"Jesus, have mercy on me!" a man who was blind called to Jesus. "What do you want?" Jesus asked the man. Then He listened to the man and healed him.

Look at people when they talk and listen to them with your heart as well as your ears. Then you will hear what they are really saying. Copy this page on another piece of paper. Color the picture, adding your hairstyle and color. Draw your nose and smile. Cut out the eyes, ears, and heart and glue them in place. Practice listening to someone with your eyes, ears, and heart. Then share Jesus' love with them.

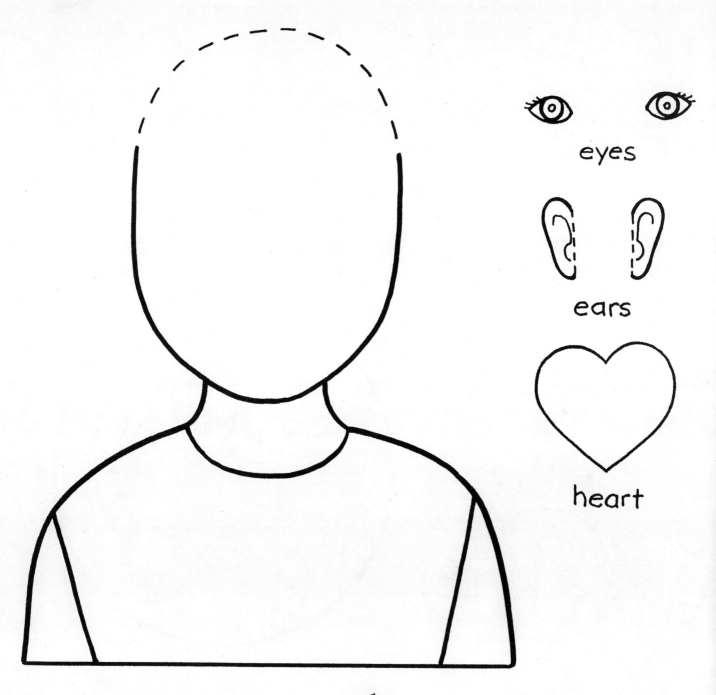

eyes

ears

heart

After Jesus and His disciples had been talking with crowds of people for a long time, they sometimes sailed away in a boat to rest. Jesus knows we need time to rest and talk to Him.

You can give some quiet time to your parents! Make some "Quiet Time" signs and hang them on the doorknob nearest them. Let Mom take a bath or a nap, or pray, without disturbing her. Let Dad rest or work on a project or read his Bible by himself.

Color and cut out the boat and flower signs. Trace the doorknob hanger on cardboard and cut out two hangers. Glue a picture on each one and slip them over doorknobs.

A QUIET TIME FOR PARENTS

Quiet!
Be Still!
Mark 4:39

Be still, and know that I am God.
Psalm 46:10

CUT OUT

On the night before He died for us, Jesus took a basin of water and a towel and washed His disciples' feet. Peter thought Jesus was too important for that job—only servants washed feet! But Jesus wanted to set an example for us in how to serve one another. The greatest service Jesus did for us is dying on the cross to pay for our sins. That great love can help us serve others.

Color and cut out the feet, soap, and Bible verse. Glue the feet and soap to a 9" colored plastic plate. Cut and fold a 2" × 4" piece of terry cloth to make a washcloth. Glue the washcloth to the plate. Glue the Bible verse on the washcloth. Punch two holes at the top of the plate. Run a ribbon through the holes to use as a hanger. Find some simple, helpful jobs you can do at home.

SERVE OTHERS

SOAP

Serve one another in love. Galatians 5:13

19

VISIT SOMEONE

When people in Jesus' day had the sickness called leprosy, they lived lonely, sad lives. No one touched them. They had to cry "Unclean!" to keep people away. One day a man sick with leprosy asked Jesus to heal him. Jesus reached out His strong hand and made him well.

Ask your parents to visit a lonely person with you. Many things can make people lonely. They may be sick. They may live alone. They may be new in your town. Take a snack and a game, a book and Bible stories. Share Jesus' love.

Color and cut out the door. After coloring the picture on page 21, fold the door on the dotted lines and glue the tab to the house.

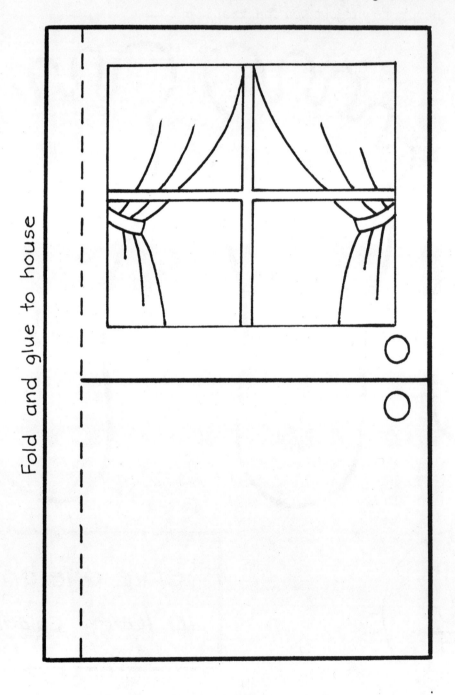

Fold and glue to house

20

WELCOME

21

WELCOME VISITORS

One day Jesus surprised His disciples. He cooked breakfast on a sandy beach! He grilled fish over a fire. His helpers felt welcomed and loved.

You can make people feel welcome in your home. Smile at visitors and say, "I'm glad you came." Color all the spaces with a dot in a bright color. Color the remaining spaces with other cheery colors. Cut out the sign to hang in your room.

Jesus enjoyed happy times with people. He visited Mary, Martha, and Lazarus in their home. He went to weddings. He ate with Matthew and Zacchaeus.

Plan a party for some friends. Invite some new people too. Make simple refreshments together. Thank God for happy times with friends.

Make copies and follow the steps to make this supersonic plane. Color, cut out, and glue on decals. See whose plane flies farthest, shortest, and funniest. Give everyone a prize for making a plane.

HAVE FUN WITH FRIENDS

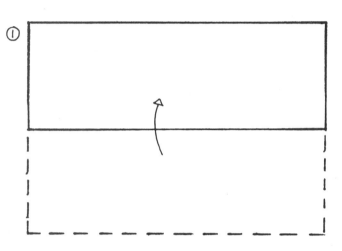

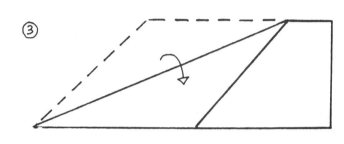

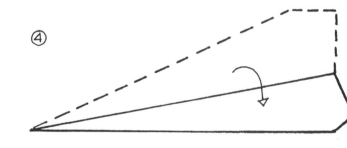

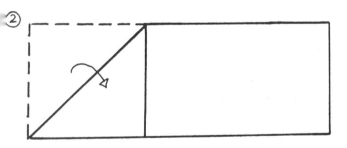

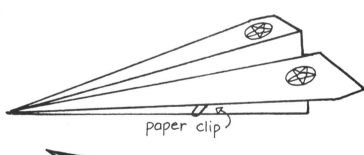

paper clip

23

INCLUDE EVERYONE

"Follow Me," Jesus told Matthew, a tax collector who was not honest. Some people thought Jesus was wrong to include Matthew. But Jesus wants all people to know that He died for their sins. If they believe in Him, they will live in heaven with Him one day.

You may know someone who always gets left out. Ask your friends to make room for that person. Color and cut out the children. Cut out a large rectangle from the side of a big grocery bag. Color an outdoor scene on it. Fold up the bottom edge of the bag about 2" and glue it at each end to make a pocket. Color grass and flowers on the pocket. Place the children in the pocket and let them play together so no one is left out.

24

glue

fold

glue

Many sick people came to a special pool in Jerusalem. When an angel stirred the water, the first person to enter the pool was healed. One man who could not walk waited for many years to be first. Someone always stepped in front of him. Jesus said, "Get up! Pick up your mat and walk." The man was healed.

Play this game and give another person the first turn. Use raisins or cereal circles to mark the hidden words.

THE · BIBLE · SAYS ·
LOVE · IS · PATIENT ·
LOVE · IS · KIND

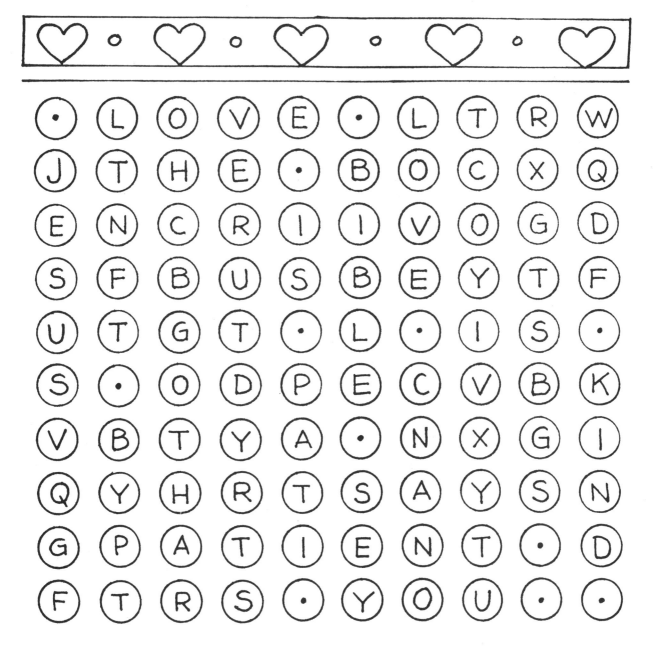

BE AN ENCOURAGER

One night a woman knelt in front of Jesus. She poured expensive perfume on His feet to show her great love for Him. The disciples grumbled. They thought she should have sold the perfume and given the money to poor people. Jesus said, "She has done a beautiful thing to Me."

Encourage others to share Jesus' love in kind, loving ways. Use the patterns to make a ribbon for someone who needs encouragement. Glue the circle on a slightly larger circle of blue construction paper. Cut, fold, and glue a strip of blue ribbon to the back. Add a yarn hanger.

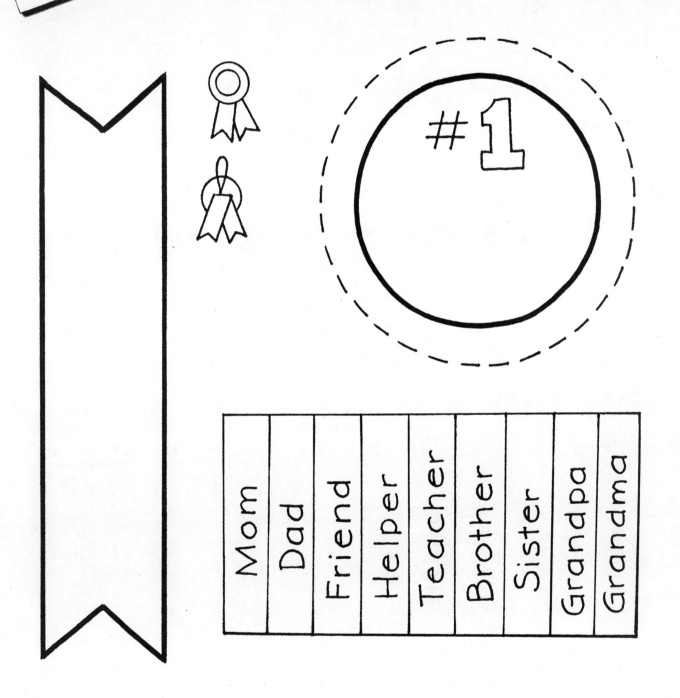

#1

Mom Dad Friend Helper Teacher Brother Sister Grandpa Grandma

26

Sick people crowded around Jesus wherever He went. Imagine how good they felt to know that Jesus cared about them. Think of someone you can cheer up with a get-well picture.

Fold 9" × 12" green construction paper in thirds, accordion style. Trace the pattern to draw leaves and a stem. Cut them out, being careful not to cut the fold. Unfold and glue on a construction paper background. Use the flower pattern to cut out several flowers. Fold as shown and staple. Glue flowers on top of stems. Add Bible verse.

Glue on picture

He cares for you.
1 Peter 5:7

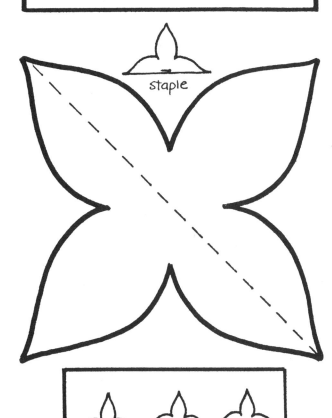

staple

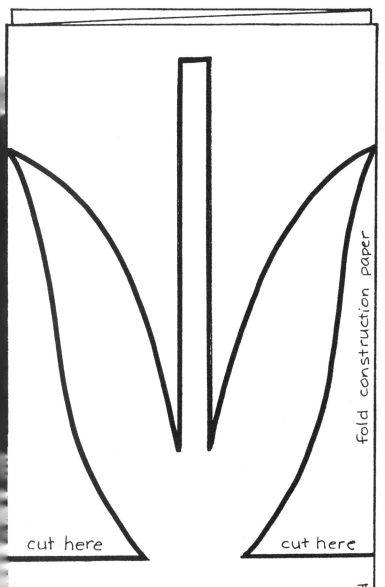

fold construction paper

cut here   cut here

fold

PLAY FAIRLY

Jesus said, "In everything, do to others what you would have them do to you" (Matthew 7:12). He will help you tell the truth and play fairly with others.

Copy two sets of the cards. Color them, cut them out, and glue them to pieces of cardboard. To play, turn cards face down. The first player turns over two cards. If the cards match, he takes another turn. If not, the second player turns two cards. The person who finds the most pairs wins.

Matthew 5:16

Luke 12:7

John 10:27

Matthew 4:19

Matthew 6:28

John 15:5

Mary, Martha, and Lazarus were good friends of Jesus. One day Lazarus became very sick. The sisters sent for Jesus, but by the time He got there, Lazarus had died. Jesus felt so sad that He cried. But then He raised Lazarus from the dead, just as we will rise one day and live with Jesus in heaven.

Visit people who are sick or lonely or sad. Tell them God loves them, and that you will pray for them. Color this cheerful picture and take it along as a gift. Color the spaces with one dot green; two dots, yellow; three dots, brown. Glue the flower on a piece of construction paper and add a yarn hanger.

COMFORT
THE
SAD

Do not let your hearts be troubled. Trust in God.   John 14:1

LEARN ABOUT DIFFERENT CULTURES

Jesus came to be the Savior of the world. He loves people from all different countries and cultures. Get to know someone who speaks a different language, or has different color skin than you do.

Trace your hand a number of times and color the hands (or use colored paper) red, white, yellow, brown, and black. Cut out the hands and arrange them in a circle on an aluminum pie pan or paper plate. Add the Bible verse in the middle. Punch two holes in the top of the pan and hang with ribbon.

You are all one in Christ Jesus.

Galatians 3:28

The wind howled. The little boat rocked and pitched. Waves crashed over the sides. "Wake up, Jesus! The boat is sinking!" the disciples shouted. They were so afraid. Jesus woke up and looked around. He told the wind to stop blowing. The sea grew calm. The disciples knew Jesus would take care of them.

You may know someone who is feeling afraid right now. Maybe a parent has lost a job. Maybe a friend's family has to move to a different city. Tell your friend or family member how Jesus calmed the storm. He will calm frightened feelings too.

Color and cut out the waves, sail, mast, flag, and Bible verse. Place the boat pattern on a folded piece of paper and cut it out.

(You may color the boat or trace it on brown construction paper.)

Glue the sail and flag to the mast. Glue the mast inside the boat. Glue the ends of the boat together. Use a paper fastener to attach the boat to a piece of 9" × 12" black construction paper. Place it about 3½" from the bottom center of the page. Glue waves on sides and bottom of the paper. Add the Bible verse. Make the boat rock. Tell the sea to be calm.

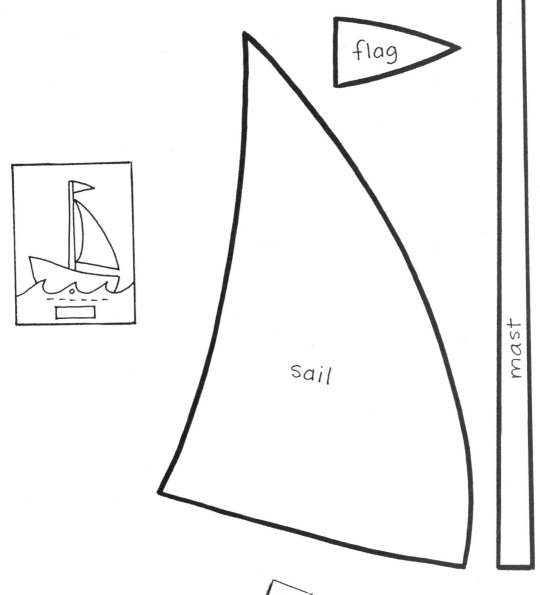

CALM SOMEONE WHO IS AFRAID

flag

mast

sail

31

"Be still!"

Mark 4: 39

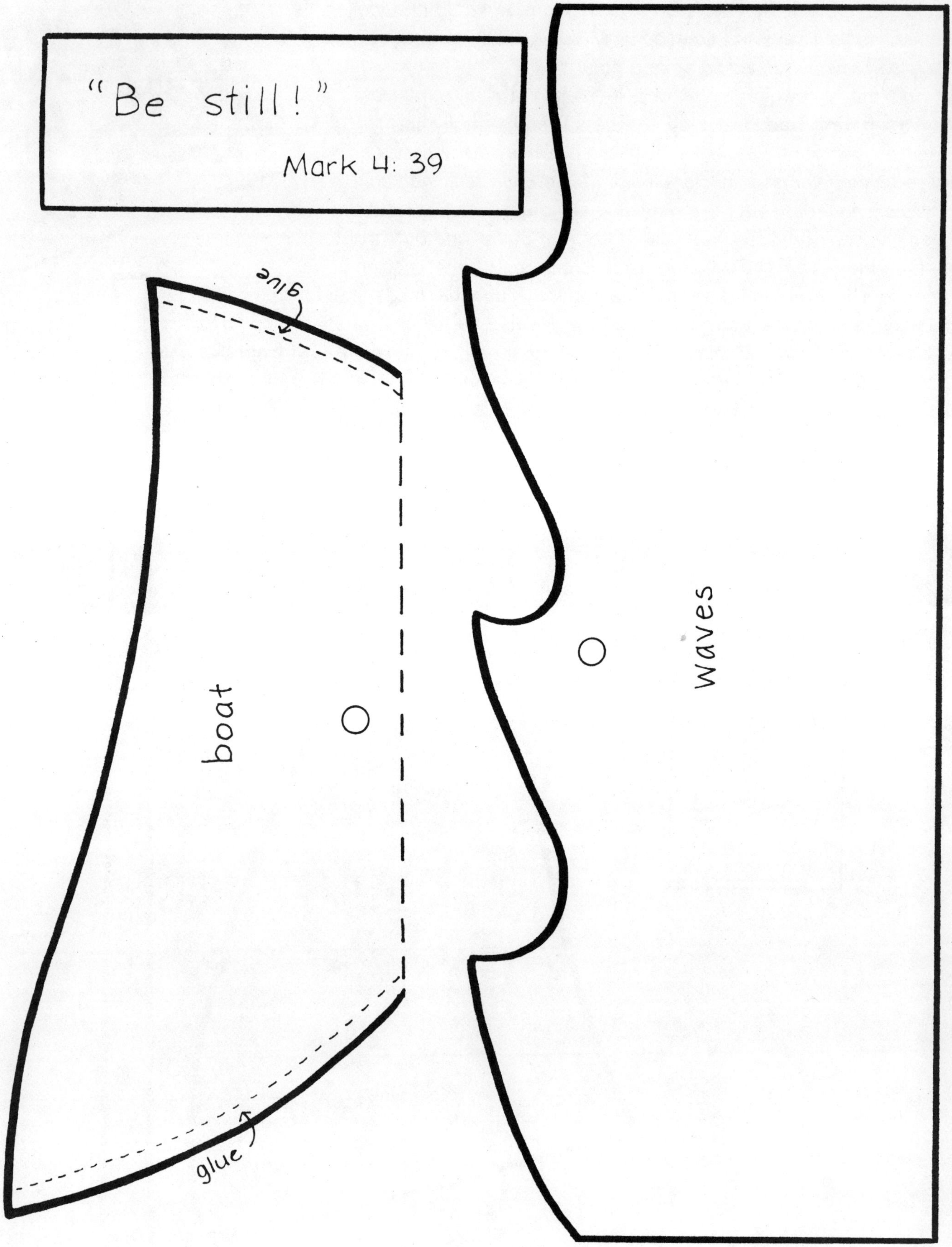

glue

boat

waves

glue

32

News spread fast: Jesus cared about people. He cared that a man was blind. He cared that people were hungry or afraid. Jesus cares about you—He cared enough to give His life for you. He will help you, no matter how you feel.

You can share Jesus' love by listening to people's feelings. You don't have to fix their problems. Just say Jesus loves them and you will pray for them. Trace the feeling words below. Then unscramble the words on the left and match them to the feeling words.

CARE HOW OTHERS FEEL

iksc

asd

rdafia

ollyen

yphpa

nhryug

sad

lonely

hungry

sick

afraid

happy

33

TRUST GOD

Jesus tells us not to worry. He tells us to look at birds. They don't save up seeds and worms. They trust God to take care of them. If God takes good care of birds, think how much more He loves and cares for us! He even sent Jesus to die for us.

If you are worried about something, remember how much God loves you. Make a beautiful bird to remind you that you don't need to worry.

Color the bird in bright colors or cut the pieces from construction paper. Place the bird's body on a piece of folded paper to cut. Cut out two each of the other patterns. Glue the head and eyes in place. Fold the wings downward on the small dashed lines. Glue a ribbon hanger in place. Glue the body together. You might want to make more birds for gifts or Christmas decorations.

Glue on ribbon tie
or elastic yarn
or thread.

34

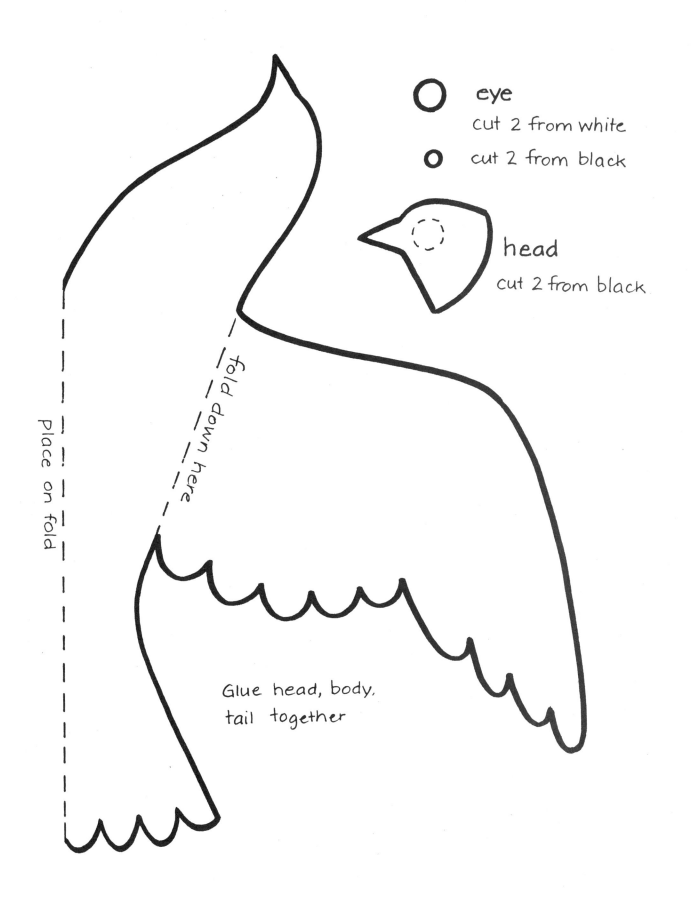

eye

cut 2 from white

cut 2 from black

head

cut 2 from black

Place on fold

fold down here

Glue head, body, tail together

LOVE GOD'S CREATION

Jesus often talked about the birds and fish and animals, and all the beautiful things we enjoy in God's creation. Talk to a friend about God's world. Remind him or her that part of God's creation is hidden under the sea. Together, color the fish in dazzling colors and cut them out. Glue your fish to a blue background. Glue on seashells and sand (or sandpaper). Think about the way God designed sea creatures to live in their ocean home. Thank God for the precious way He designed you.

36

Jesus honored His parents. He helped them and obeyed them. Even as He suffered for us on the cross, He made sure His mother would be taken care of.

Thank God for giving you loving parents. Ask Him to help you honor them as Jesus did. Make some coupons for your mom or dad. Write down, or draw pictures of, things you can do for them. Include snacks you can make, chores you can do, errands you can run. Don't forget to give them a big hug.

HONOR YOUR PARENTS

♡ I'm glad you're my _____.
♡ Present this coupon for one:
♡
♡   Love, _____

♡ I'm glad you're my _____.
♡ Present this coupon for one:
♡
♡   Love, _____

♡ I'm glad you're my _____.
♡ Present this coupon for one:
♡
♡   Love, _____

♡ I'm glad you're my _____.
♡ Present this coupon for one:
♡
♡   Love, _____

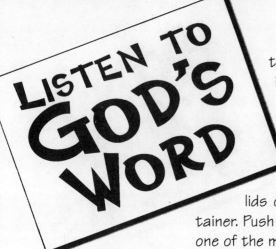

LISTEN TO GOD'S WORD

We learn about God's love by studying His Word. When you read the Bible or a Bible storybook with your parents, learn about Jesus in Sunday school, and hear your pastor preach about God's love, the Holy Spirit helps you listen to God speak.

The next time you read God's Word or a story about Jesus, wear your heavenly earphones! They will help you stay tuned to God's voice. Cut out the "God speaks" and "I listen" circles and glue them to the bottoms of two margarine tubs. (Leave lids on tubs.) Remove the lid from a used half-gallon ice cream container. Push out the top. Cut the rim as shown. Tape each end of the strip to one of the margarine tubs.

 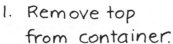 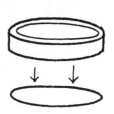  

1. Remove top from container.

2. Push out top of lid.

3. Make one cut in rim to open it into a U-shape.

4. Tape a small margarine tub to each end of rim.

5. Cut and glue the circles on the tubs.

God Speaks

I Listen

Jesus said that our life with Him is like a grapevine. He is the vine, we are the branches. Jesus gives us everything we need to live—especially forgiveness for our sins and the promise of new life with Him forever.

Grapes can remind us of the good fruit that God's Holy Spirit grows in our lives as we learn about Jesus. You can learn about this good fruit—love, joy, peace, kindness, goodness, and more—by reading Galatians 5:22–23.

Use torn paper to make a grape picture. Tear about 30 grapes from purple construction paper. Tear leaves from green paper. Glue the grapes and leaves on white paper. Add green curly ribbon for tendrils. Write the Bible verse on your picture.

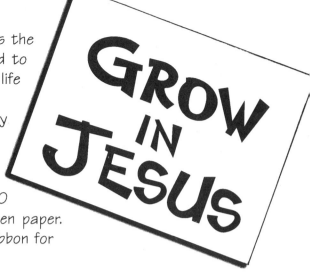

"I am the vine; you are the branches. If a man remains in Me and I in him, he will bear much fruit."

John 15:5

TALK TO GOD AT ALL TIMES

Jesus talked to His Father all day long. He prayed before the sun rose. He prayed during hot, busy days. He prayed through still, dark nights. Jesus knew that our Father always listens to us when we pray.

You can talk to God throughout your day. Tell Him you love Him. Tell Him you are sorry for the things you do wrong. Ask Him to help you with your problems. Thank Him for being such a great God.

Color and cut out the clock and hands. Glue the clock on a piece of construction paper. Attach the hands with a paper fastener. Move the hands to show the times you do different things throughout the day. Talk with your family about what you might pray about at each time.

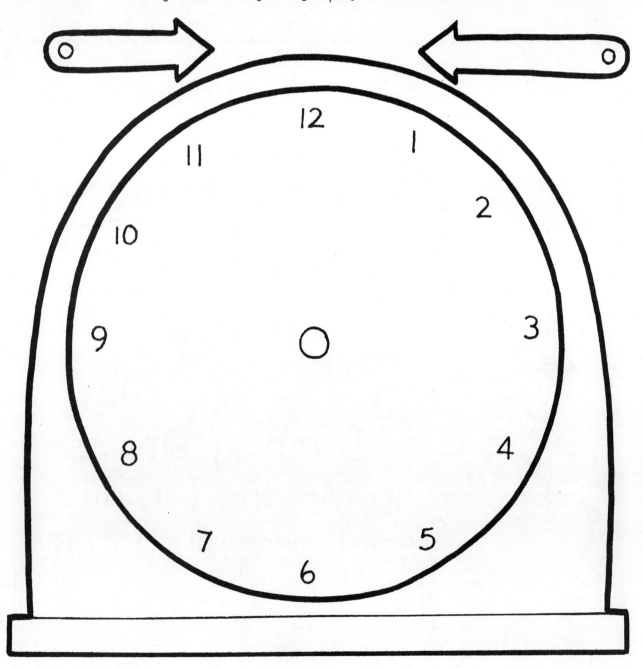

Jesus loved going to church and talking with teachers about God's love, even when He was a boy. When He grew to be a man He often taught people in the big temple church in Jerusalem about God's plan for our salvation.

Invite a friend to go to church with you. Tell your friends how happy you feel to go to God's house.

Cut out the church pattern and place it on a piece of folded white paper. Cut out the church as indicated. Cut up 1" from the bottom of the fold. Fold up the bottom edge of the paper and glue at each end to make a pocket on the front of the church and on the inside. Color the outside of the church to look like your church. Color the inside of the church to look like the inside of your church. Color and cut out the children. Put them in the pockets to help them walk to church, then go inside the church.

WORSHIP GOD IN CHURCH

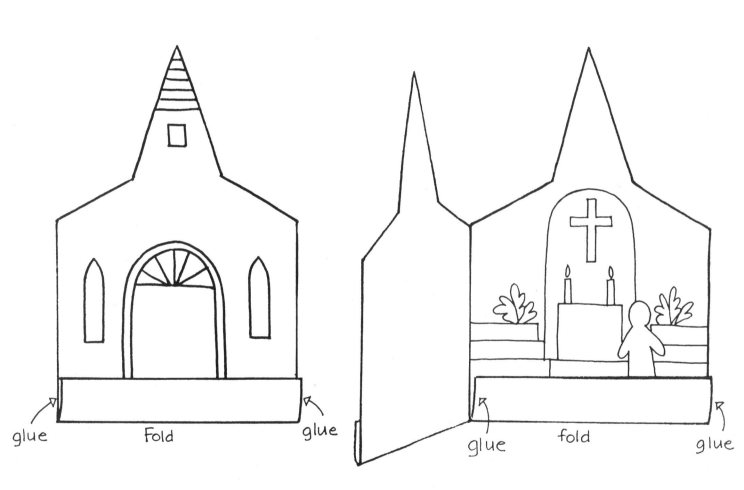

glue   Fold   glue

glue   fold   glue

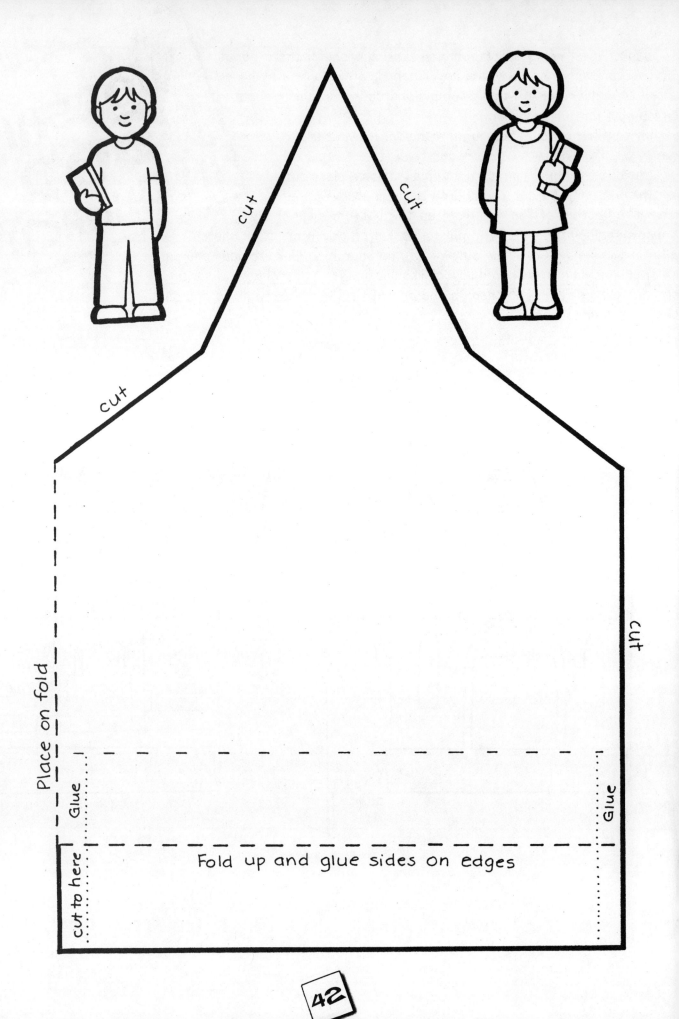

cut

cut

cut

cut

Place on fold

Glue

Glue

cut to here

Fold up and glue sides on edges

42

When Jesus left His disciples to go back to heaven, He promised to send the Holy Spirit to help them. God's Holy Spirit began living in you when you were baptized. He helps your faith in Jesus grow and grow. He helps you reflect Jesus' love so others can see you acting in loving ways. Color the mirror frame. Cut a circle of foil and glue it in the center. Cut out the words and glue them in the center of the mirror. Fold a sheet of construction paper in half. Glue it on the back of the mirror as a stand.

REFLECT JESUS' LOVE

cut out

Let others see Jesus in you.

SHARE THE GOOD NEWS

Everything that Jesus did pointed to the Good News that He is our Savior from sin and death. Share that Good News with friends and neighbors.

Make this heart-shaped basket to give to someone who needs to know Jesus' love. Fold two pieces of construction paper and cut off the top outer corner of each, as shown. Place the folded papers together to make a heart. Glue in place. Add your picture and a Good News message such as "Jesus loves you." Cut flowers from magazines and glue them on chenille sticks to place in the basket. You might include a picture of Jesus or a Bible verse too. Hang the basket on someone's doorknob, or give it to someone, along with a hug.

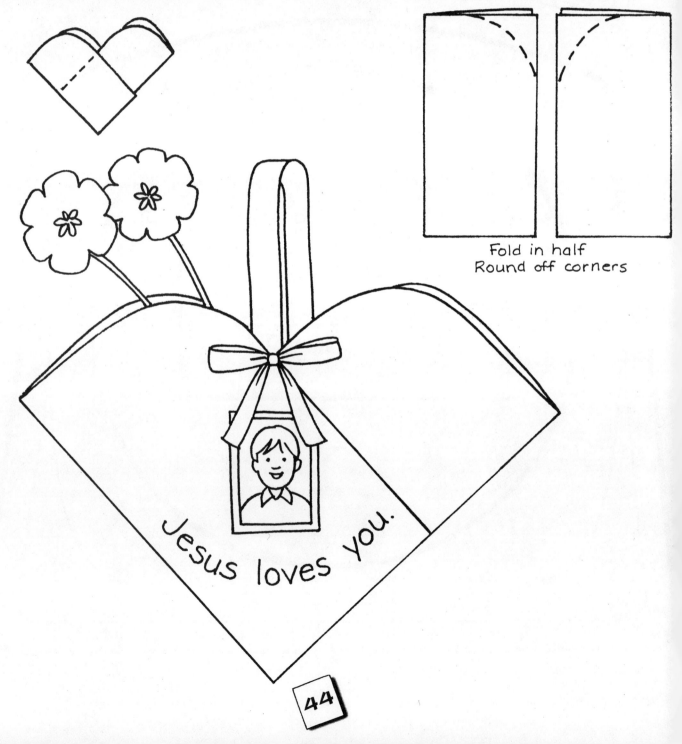

Fold in half
Round off corners

Jesus loves you.

Jesus lived His whole life for us. He lived a perfect life, then died on the cross to pay for our sins. He rose again, just as we will rise one day and live with Him in heaven. God's Holy Spirit helps us live in Jesus each day, thanking Him for all He has done for us. Write a thank-You prayer to Jesus on the lines below.

THANK YOU, JESUS

Dear Jesus,
Thank You for

Amen.

PRAISE GOD

You have seen how Jesus loves you every minute of your life. He will always keep you close to Him. Draw a picture about Jesus' love in the frame. Fold a piece of drawing paper in half. Place the dashed line of the pattern on the fold. Cut out the person and color it to look like you. Put the picture you drew in "your" hands and feet as shown.